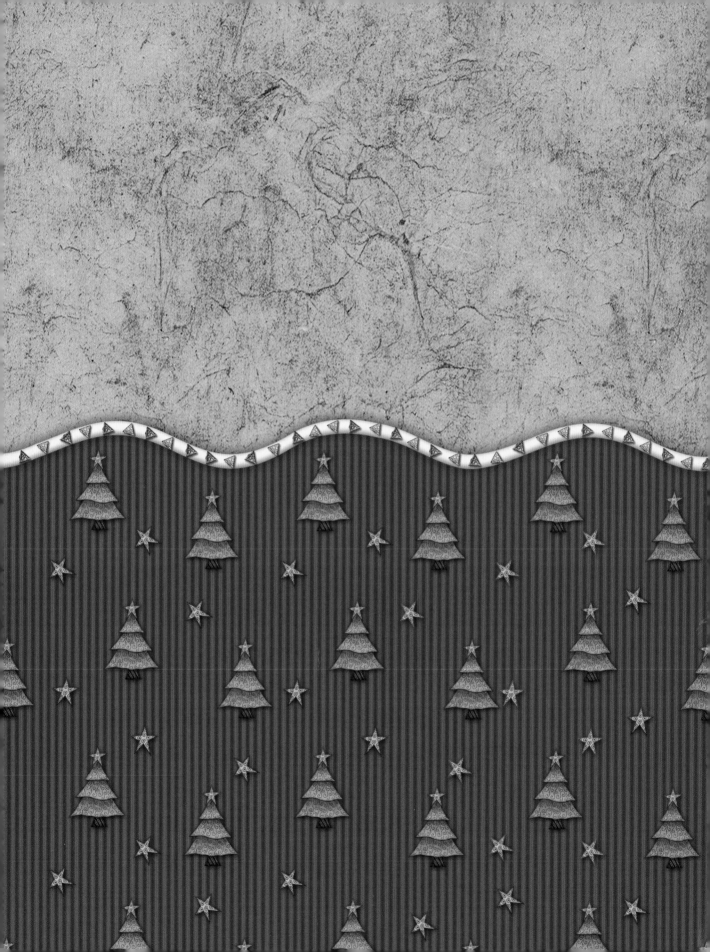

The ADVENTure of Christmas

Helping Children Find Jesus in our Holiday Traditions

A Mom's Guide

by Lisa Whelchel
Artwork by Jeannie Mooney

Multnomah Gifts
Multnomah® Publishers *Sisters, Oregon*

It is with great joy that I am able
to dedicate this book to my father,
Jimmy Lee Whelchel.
I am grateful for the wonderful childhood
memories he provided, *especially* the ones
surrounding Christmas.

I am also indebted to my spiritual father,
Pastor Jack Hayford,
for hosting the best birthday party in town each Christmas
and for teaching us to celebrate the celebration.

The ADVENTure of Christmas
published by Multnomah Gifts®,
a division of Multnomah® Publishers, Inc.

© 2004 by Lisa Whelchel

Artwork © by Jeannie Mooney. All rights reserved.

International Standard Book Number: 1-59052-089-0

Design by Koechel Peterson & Assoc., Inc., Minneapolis, Minnesota

Unless otherwise indicated, Scripture quotations are taken from:
Holy Bible, New Living Translation © 1996. Used by permission of Tyndale House Publishers, Inc.
All rights reserved.
Other versions include:
The Holy Bible, New International Version (NIV) © 1973, 1984 by International Bible Society,
used by permission of Zondervan Publishing House.
The Holy Bible, New King James Version (NKJV) © 1984 by Thomas Nelson, Inc.
The Holy Bible, King James Version (KJV)
The New Testament in Modern English, Revised Edition (Phillips) © 1958, 1960, 1972 by J. B. Phillips.
The Message by Eugene H. Peterson, Copyright © 1993, 1994, 1995, 1996, 2000. Used by permission of
NavPress Publishing Group. All rights reserved.

Multnomah Publishers, Inc., has made every effort to provide proper and accurate source attribution for
all selections used in this book. Should any attribution be found to be incorrect, the publisher welcomes
written documentation supporting correction for subsequent printings. We gratefully acknowledge the
cooperation of other publishers and individuals who have granted permission for use of their material.

Multnomah is a trademark of Multnomah Publishers, Inc., and is registered in the U.S. Patent and
Trademark Office. The colophon is a trademark of Multnomah Publishers, Inc.

Printed in China

For Information:
MULTNOMAH PUBLISHERS, INC. • P.O. BOX 1720 • SISTERS, OR 97759

05 06 07 08 09 10 11—10 9 8 7 6 5 4 3

Table of Contents

INTRODUCTION

If you were to ask my children, "What is the meaning of Christmas?" they would dutifully reply, "The birth of Jesus." But I know them better than that. To these three little ones, Christmas is really about opening presents, baking cookies, decorating the tree, and stringing twinkle lights with Daddy.

Sure, we read the Christmas story, attend candlelight services, and quote the obligatory "Jesus is the reason for the season" while simultaneously wiping tears from their eyes and drool off their chins in the Barbie aisle of Toys "R" Us. But if you could see into my children's hearts, you would understand that, to them, Christmas is not only about the birth of Jesus—it's also about *celebrating* the birth of Jesus.

I recently learned that celebrating Christmas is not far from the heart of God, either. Feeling like Jesus had gotten lost in the frenzy of the holiday season, I asked the Lord to show me what I could do to teach my children the true meaning of Christmas. I was caught off-guard when He simply replied, "Don't do anything differently. Look in the middle of the celebration and you will find Me."

He was right, of course. I didn't need to orchestrate moments to pontificate with my kids about "the commercialization of Christmas." Instead, Jesus was beckoning me to come to the party and bring the kids. In doing so, we ran into Him at school, in our living room, even at the mall. He hid in the lights, the carols, and the cards. He was there when we dressed the evergreen tree, when Dad dressed up in a red suit, and when we ate turkey and dressing! We got caught up in all the trappings of Christmas only to discover that it was neither the enemy nor the world that set the bait.

Now it is my desire to lure parents into the hustle and bustle of Christmas and then set them free to join their children in the celebration—guilt-free. On each day of the traditional Advent, the twenty-four days preceding Christmas, we will explore together a different aspect of the Christmas celebration. It's amazing how short a distance you have to go to find Jesus in our present-day symbols and traditions. We will encounter the true meaning of Christmas in such unlikely places as a candy cane, a fruitcake, and the partridge in a pear tree. We will rediscover the significance of Santa Claus, tree ornaments, and even the colors of Christmas.

I know that my own children (one in particular) seem to hear better with their hands. I can tell them something all day long, but if they get the chance to *do* something with that information, then it is usually theirs for life. With that in mind, I've included fun and simple activities each day to help you teach the profound truth of Jesus' birth in a way that will remain in your child's heart long after the Christmas decorations are back in the attic.

Having been an actress since I was a child, I've often wished there was a script for life. It would be so much easier. Many times I've known *what* I wanted to say to my children but just didn't know *how* to say it. Just in case you have ever felt the same way, I've written a short "script" for each day to help you easily share these truths with your family.

Of course, you could read the book aloud to your children, but the truth is, they would much rather hear from you than from me. I suggest that first you read the history and application of each of these symbols and traditions. Then look for one of those "teachable moments" and ask your children a few of the scripted questions. (You, the oh-so-wise mommy, will just happen to be ready with the answers.)

Imagine the delightful conversations you're going to have this Christmas! Keep the book handy and while wrapping gifts, icing cookies, hanging tinsel, and singing carols, look behind every song, every story, for the Best of All Stories. May the seeking—and the finding—bring you and your family much joy.

ADVENT WREATH

It's exciting to have someone special come visit, isn't it? You clean the house, make special meals, and maybe even count the days! Well, that's what Advent is all about. The word *advent* means "to come," and it refers to Jesus' coming to earth as a baby on Christmas Day. The season of Advent is all about looking forward to celebrating the day when our almighty God stepped into history as a human being.

In days past, Christians would prepare their hearts to celebrate the arrival of God's Son by tidying their lives up a bit. They would remember the poor and perhaps even fast. They understood that when the holiday festivities began there would be plenty of time for enjoying delicious food and exchanging gifts. But it was important to begin the reception by focusing on the reason for the party.

Of course, this is also a good time to look inside ourselves and see if there is anything that needs a little cleaning up as we anticipate the arrival of Jesus' second coming.

One of the ways we can join in the celebration is with an Advent wreath. This circle of evergreen boughs reminds us of God's forever love, a love that has no beginning and no end. Four candles—three purple and one pink—stand amid the greenery. A white candle stands in the center.

The first purple candle is called Prophecy, or the Hope candle; it invites us to thank God for the hope we have in Jesus, the prophesied Messiah. The second purple candle is called Bethlehem, or Peace. In Bethlehem, the Prince of Peace was born so that we sinners could be at peace with our holy God.

The pink Shepherd's candle, or Joy, celebrates the good tidings of great joy that is for all people: Christ is born! The final purple candle is called Angel, or Love. Joining with the heavenly hosts that first Christmas night, we say, "Glory to God in the highest, and on earth peace, good will toward men" (Luke 2:14, KJV).

Love has entered our world through the birth of Jesus, represented by the white Christ candle. The baby came to die on a cross as punishment for our sins. That's amazing love! Something indeed worth taking four weeks to think about.

Celebrate with an Advent Wreath

Purchase an Advent wreath, or make one with a circle of evergreen boughs and five candles. The first purple candle is lighted on the fourth Sunday before Christmas. On the next Sunday, light both the first and second purple candles. Two Sundays before Christmas, light the first two purple candles as well as the pink candle. The last purple candle is lighted with the other three on the Sunday before Christmas. On Christmas Day, light all four candles and the white Christ candle.

Advent Calendar of Kisses

Another fun way to anticipate the coming of Christmas is with an Advent calendar. You can make your own with twenty-five chocolate kisses, a few feet of plastic wrap, and some curling ribbon. Simply roll out the plastic wrap, line up twenty-five chocolate kisses one inch apart, and fold both sides of the plastic wrap over the chocolate. Cut twenty-six pieces of curling ribbon, each approximately six inches long, and tie each piece in a knot between the kisses. Tie one longer ribbon at the top and hang from a doorknob or a hook in the kitchen. Beginning on the morning of December 1, exchange one kiss from your child for a "kiss" from the Advent calendar as you count down the days until Christmas together!

TEACHABLE MOMENTS

- *"Do you know what Advent is and why it is good to celebrate it?"* (Explain what the word advent means and how we can prepare our hearts for Christmas.)

- *"Did you know that each of those pretty candles has a name and a special meaning?"* (Share the names and meanings of each candle.)

- *"Many families celebrate Advent with a wreath and light the candles on special days. Would you like to do that?"* (Make or buy an Advent wreath and help your child light the candles on each special Sunday this Christmas.)

THE CHRISTMAS TREE

It is said that in the seventh century a zealous young English missionary was the first person to use the evergreen tree as a symbol for God. Winfrid, who would later become known as Saint Boniface, used the tree as an object lesson. He taught that each point on the triangular-shaped tree represented a different Person of the Holy Trinity—Father, Son, and Holy Spirit.

Legend has it that one day Winfrid came upon a group of men offering a sacrifice to an oak tree as an act of worship. So angered was he by this idolatry that Winfrid swung his ax and felled the oak tree with one mighty blow. According to the tale, a fir tree eventually grew from the stump of the oak. Struck by this occurrence, the missionary proclaimed that the tiny new tree represented Jesus' victory over death on the cross and the eternal life made available to us by the King of kings.

The Christmas tree is a beautiful reminder of why Jesus was born in the first place—to die for you and me. "He himself bore our sins in his body on the tree, so that we might die to sins and live for righteousness" (1 Peter 2:24, NIV). As we put up the Christmas tree in our homes, it can only deepen our joy if we remember His death at this time of His birth. It is because He died for us that we can receive the eternal life represented by the evergreen boughs.

Have you ever noticed that the boughs of your tree extend out like the arms of Jesus stretched upon the cross as He offered His life to anyone who would come to Him in faith? And your Christmas tree is very definitely pointing toward heaven and, as Jesus did with His words and His actions, drawing our attention to the Father who loves us.

So when you stand before your Christmas tree, stand tall, as the tree does, and be a witness for Jesus. Let it direct your attention to the Father above. Fix your eyes on Jesus, then open your arms wide to touch others with His Spirit of love. Then you, too, will be pointing people toward heaven—and to life beyond the power of death.

- *Why do you think the Christmas tree is the main holiday decoration?*
  (Talk about how it represents the tree Jesus died on, which is why He was born in the first place.)
- *Can you find other ways the tree might remind us of Jesus?*
  (Point out the ways the tree illustrates Jesus.)
- *Could we use the tree to tell other people about Jesus?*
  (Share the legend of Winfrid and the pagan worshipers.)

Animal Christmas Tree

Find a tree in a forest (or your backyard, if you live in the urban jungle) and decorate it for the animals. String berries, pieces of fruit, and popcorn and drape them around the tree. Poke pieces of bread and cake on the branches. Hang birdseed bells, or make your own by smearing peanut butter on empty toilet paper rolls and then rolling them in sunflower seeds and nuts. Watch the animals feast away with your children.

At this glorious time of Christmas

Peace on Earth

Christmas Cone-ifer

What you'll need:

    Sugar ice-cream cones
    Green cake frosting
    Miniature M&Ms

Directions:

Let your children spread the green frosting over the entire sugar cone. Turn the cone upside down and decorate it with the miniature M&Ms. Sing "O Christmas Tree" and then eat it!

LIGHTS ON THE TREE

As the story goes, a professor named Martin Luther was walking alone through a forest one December night in the early 1500s. As he made his way home, the stars seemed to twinkle with an unusual brightness against the velvety blackness of the clear night sky. In fact, when he passed under the rustling branches of the evergreens, it seemed to him that miniature stars were dancing in the trees all around him.

It wasn't the sudden gust of cold wind that took the professor's breath away; it was the unexpected wave of worship that caused him to shiver. Luther was overwhelmed by the awesome beauty of God's creation.

The legend goes on to tell how Luther chopped down a small fir tree and set it up in his family's living area. He desperately wanted to somehow capture that moment in the starlit forest. Yet as he attempted to describe the beauty he had seen, words completely failed him.

Suddenly Luther had an idea. He went through his house and gathered up all the burning candles. One by one, he carefully placed them on the branches of the tree, and the little fir in the middle of the Luther home began to dance with twinkling lights. This wise papa's plan had worked! The Luther children's eyes were suddenly opened to the meaning of Psalm 19:1: "The heavens tell of the glory of God. The skies display his marvelous craftsmanship."

My Very Own Christmas Tree

Purchase a small Christmas tree and place it in your child's room. Together string a strand of Christmas lights around the tree. This will not only be her special tree but it will also act as a night-light during the holiday season.

Christmas Tree Cake with Flaming Stars

What you will need:

One 13x9-inch sheet cake (ready-made or purchased)
One cake board to display cake
Scissors
Green cake frosting
Cake knife for spreading frosting
Small amount of red and blue frosting
Sugar cubes
Small bottle of peppermint extract

Directions:

1. Transfer the sheet cake onto the cake board. Trace a simple Christmas tree pattern on top of your cake and carefully cut away the surrounding cake. Be careful not to damage the large cut-away pieces, because you are going to use them later.

2. Carefully frost the Christmas-tree cake with the green frosting.

3. Arrange the sugar cubes on the surface to look like lights on a tree.

4. Cut leftover cake into small square- and rectangular-shaped "boxes" and frost them with the red and blue frosting.

5. Pipe a frosting ribbon on the "gifts" to make them look like presents. Arrange them around the bottom of the cake.

6. For a special effect, infuse each sugar cube with a few drops of the peppermint extract just prior to igniting.

7. Turn off lights and use a match to carefully ignite the extract on each "star," moving quickly from cube to cube. Each star will burn with a pretty blue flame for about a minute.

TEACHABLE MOMENTS

- *"Who in the world came up with the idea of putting lights on a tree?"*
  (Share the story of Martin Luther's evening walk through the forest.)

- *"Do you think it might have been dangerous to put candles on a tree?"*
  (Talk about how to be safe during the holidays by keeping the tree watered and not playing with candles or electric lights.)

- *"When you look at the stars in the sky, what do you think about?"*
  (End the conversation by teaching your child that we can learn a lot about God, the Creator of the world, by looking at His creation.)

ORNAMENTS ON THE TREE

In medieval Europe, plays were performed throughout the year based on the lives of Bible characters. December 24 was declared Adam and Eve's Day and the setting of this day's drama was the Garden of Eden. Remember what happened? The serpent tempted Eve to disobey God and eat the forbidden fruit. And she did. The play ended with God sending Adam and Eve out of paradise as a consequence of their sin.

There was only one minor problem in staging this drama: finding a fruit tree in winter! Some Renaissance stage director must have discovered that with a little smoke and mirrors, he could turn a pine tree strung with apples into the Tree of Knowledge of Good and Evil. This "costumed" tree delighted the audience and became the star of the show.

The decorated evergreen delighted audiences, even upstaging the actors. Years after the medieval plays were no longer performed, German families continued to decorate their own evergreens with shiny red apples on December 24 and to call them "paradise trees."

Through the years, the decorations became more and more elaborate. Mothers hid gingerbread cookies in the branches. Nuts dipped in sugar were nestled among the pine needles. Fruits and vegetables formed from marzipan candy hung from the boughs. The family Christmas tree became so sugar-coated, it was often appropriately referred to as the "sugar tree."

But no matter how sweet the treats, the most important ornaments were tiny round wafers of bread hidden among the other decorations. These thin biscuits represented the body of Christ that was broken on the cross for our sins. And so hidden among the forbidden fruit, through which death entered the world, were signs of Jesus Christ, the One who gives us eternal life.

As we decorate our Christmas tree we should be reminded of Romans 5:19— "Because one person [Adam] disobeyed God, many people became sinners. But because one other person [Jesus] obeyed God, many people will be made right in God's sight."

No-Bake Spiced Dough Ornaments

This is a fun and safe craft to make with your child. Kids love getting their hands all messy. Just remind them that they can't lick their fingers. (Unless, of course, your tot has been talking nonstop and you think the glue might bring a little peace and quiet.)

Ingredients:

1 cup ground cinnamon

1 tablespoon ground cloves

1 tablespoon ground ginger

1 tablespoon ground nutmeg

1 cup applesauce

2 tablespoon white craft glue

Food coloring (optional)

A few tablespoons of all-purpose flour

Directions:

1. Combine the cinnamon, cloves, ginger, and nutmeg in a mixing bowl.
2. Add the applesauce and glue.
3. Have your child help you work in all the ingredients with your hands until ingredients are mixed thoroughly.
4. If desired, divide into portions and mix a few drops of food coloring into each.
5. Roll the dough out on a lightly floured surface to approximately ¼-inch thickness.
6. Cut dough with cookie cutters into various shapes.
7. Bore a hole in the top of each ornament (a drinking straw works well for this).
8. Lay the ornaments out flat to dry at room temperature for 3 to 5 days, turning over often. (If you or your child runs out of patience, you can always speed up the process by popping these in a 200°F oven for 1 hour.)
9. When they are completely dry, thread short lengths of ribbon or string through the hole in each ornament.

TEACHABLE MOMENTS

- *"What in the world would make a person hang things all over a tree?"*

  (Tell your children about the medieval plays and the very first "paradise tree.")

- *"Some of our family ornaments look good enough to eat. Did you know that a long time ago you really could eat the ornaments?"*

  (Describe some of the ornaments that moms used to hang on the "sugar tree.")

- *"Why do you think moms would hang little bread crackers on the tree along with all the yummy goodies?"*

  (Explain that at the very first "communion," or "Eucharist," Christ referred to the bread as His body broken on the cross for our salvation.)

THE CANDY CANE

The candy cane has come a long way since its days as a pacifier. It started out as a simple white stick of sugar that parents gave babies to suck on when they got fussy. During the 1670s, a nameless German choirmaster had the bright idea of bending the sticks into the shape of a shepherd's crook. As they entered the cathedral, each tiny tot was handed a "candy cane," just in case they became quite vocal about their lack of interest in the Christmas pageant.

Hundreds of years later—or so the legend goes—a candy maker in Indiana decided to improve upon the choirmaster's sweet idea by tying the treats in with the real meaning of Christmas. First, he added a large red stripe as a symbol of the blood Jesus shed on the cross. The confectioner added smaller red stripes to represent both the lashes from the soldiers' whips across Jesus' back and the promise that "by His stripes we are healed" (Isaiah 53:5, NKJV). The white color reminded children that Jesus lived a life completely without sin.

Peppermint flavoring was added that called to mind hyssop, the Old Testament plant used in sacrifices, because Jesus was the perfect sacrifice for our sins. The candy's hardness declares that Jesus is the Rock of our salvation.

The bent cane already reminded folks of the shepherds of Judea—the first people to learn that the Savior had been born. And if you turn the candy cane upside down? It forms the letter *J*—for Jesus.

Isn't it wonderful that every candy cane you share is a story waiting to be told and an invitation to "taste and see that the LORD is good" (Psalm 34:8, NIV)?

Candy Cane Science Experiment

Have your older children meet you in the kitchen for a chemistry lesson.

Ingredients:

½ cup water

3 cups granulated sugar

¾ cup corn syrup

¼ teaspoon cream of tartar

1 teaspoon peppermint flavoring

¾ teaspoon red food coloring

Candy thermometer

Directions:

1. Combine water, sugar, corn syrup, and cream of tartar in a medium saucepan. Whisk together over low heat until the sugar is completely dissolved.

2. Divide the liquid between two saucepans and bring both to a boil, but don't stir until the temperature of each registers 280°F.

3. Add ½ teaspoon of peppermint flavoring to each pan and stir.

4. Add the red food coloring to only one of the pans and stir.

5. Remove pans from heat and cool.

6. After the contents of both pans have cooled enough to handle, stretch and pull the mixture, like taffy, forming into ropes of red and white. Then twist them around each other again and again.

7. Form the intertwined red and white ropes into the shape of a shepherd's staff.

8. Allow them to harden on an oiled surface.

9. Share the candy canes with younger siblings or neighborhood children and tell them the story it preaches.

TEACHABLE MOMENTS

- *"Can you believe the first candy cane was used as a pacifier for babies?"*

  (Share the story of the German choirmaster who used the sugar cane to keep tiny tots quiet during the Christmas play.)

- *"Let's see if we can guess what each part of the candy cane represents."*

  (Point out each of the symbols hidden within the candy cane.)

- *"Why do you think the candy maker created the candy cane?"*

  (Tell the story about how the candy maker in Indiana used his talents to tell others about Jesus.)

The Legend of the Candy Cane

Once upon a time ... a candy maker created the perfect candy to symbolize the true meaning of Christmas. It was the candy cane. The white stripes would stand for the purity of Christ and his Virgin birth. The red stripes would signify the pain & death Jesus endured on our behalf. The hook shape would also be a reminder to all people of the name Jesus & his role as Good Shepherd.

© jeannie mooney

Reindeer Evangelists

Transform candy canes into reindeer, tie a copy of *The Candy Cane Story* to one of the antlers, and pass these treats to friends or classmates.

Things you'll need for each reindeer:

One 6-inch cellophane-wrapped candy cane

8 inches of ribbon

1 pair of wiggly eyes

1 small red pom-pom

Two 18-inch brown pipe cleaners

White craft glue

Scissors

Directions:

1. Glue wiggly eyes on the rounded crook of the candy cane.

2. Glue red pom-pom on the face for a nose.

3. Tie ribbon into a bow on the straight part of the candy cane.

4. Cut one of the pipe cleaners in half.

5. Wrap the full-sized pipe cleaner around the crook of the candy cane, twisting once at the bottom to secure, then back up into the air; the two points should now be standing straight up.

6. Twist one of the short pipe cleaners around the middle of the left antler to create the "points." Repeat with the remaining cut piece of pipe cleaner for the right antler.

7. Manipulate the pipe cleaners to look like antlers. (When finished, each antler will have three points.)

THE STAR

When we place a star high atop the Christmas tree, we are remembering a star from long ago—a wondrous sign in the deep heavens that drew seekers on a long and dangerous journey across the known world. Magi from the east came asking, "Where is the one who has been born king of the Jews? We saw his star in the east and have come to worship him" (Matthew 2:2, NIV).

For thousands of years, men have considered the brilliant handiwork of God displayed in the ordering of the heavens. With the help of computers, astronomers today can actually approximate what the Judean sky might have looked like more than two thousand years ago. Some have suggested that the star of Bethlehem was a conjunction of planets that came together in the sky in a rare, brilliant convergence.

How then did its light shine directly on the house where the Christ child was staying with His mother, as Scripture tells us? In fact, it was nothing less than a miracle. No further explanation needed! God, who has directed the course of history from the moment He created the heavens and the earth, wanted to set the stage for the most momentous night our fallen, unhappy planet has ever known. So He placed a spotlight in the heavens to shine on the real star of the show: a humble Child who was more than a child.

The Bible says of the Magi that "the sight of the star filled them with indescribable joy" (Matthew 2:10, Phillips).

We, too, can experience that joy as we fix the gaze of our hearts on Jesus, the Bright and Morning Star.

joyous night

The Star Sewn Brightly in the Night

Need something to keep those little hands busy while your big hands are busy? With only a few minutes of preparation, you can keep your child occupied long enough to wrap a few presents, bake a dozen cookies, or fold a load of laundry. (I'd opt for the cookies if I were you!)

What you'll need:

Black construction paper

Gold cord or yarn

A hole punch

Directions:

Draw a large star on the black paper and have your child cut it out. Help your child punch holes ½-inch apart along the edges. Thread the gold cord or yarn through the first hole. Tape the end of the cord to the back of the star. Show your child how to "sew" the cord along the perimeter of the star. When finished, tie the two ends together with a small knot. If there is still laundry left to do, encourage your child to use the star as a template and create one all by himself.

TEACHABLE MOMENTS

- *"Stars live in the sky, not on top of trees! Why do you think we put one on our Christmas tree?"*
  (Rehearse the familiar story of the wise men following the star to Bethlehem.)

- *"Do you think we can still look to the stars for direction today?"*
  (Enjoy a wonder-filled conversation about sailors and scientists and constellations. Include a simple caution against looking for direction for the future through planets and horoscopes.)

- *"How in the world did that famous star stay in one place for so long?"*
  (Talk about the fact that we can understand many things in the Bible but there are just some things we can't explain and that is because God is God and we are not. And that's okay.)

Merry Christmas. Happy holidays. Season's greetings. So many good wishes, but do we really know what we're saying? (Or not saying?) "Season's greetings!" is about as bland a salutation as we could ever receive. What does it mean? "Hello, in the middle of winter!"?

"Happy holidays!" comes a little closer to having some kind of heartfelt meaning. Originally, the wish was for "Happy holy days," those days set aside specifically for worshiping God. Sometime in the sixteenth century, the term started referring to any day off from work that was devoted to rest and recreation. The word became holiday, and now the phrase seems to mean "Enjoy this time of year—whatever you're celebrating!"

Then there's the shorthand "Merry X-mas," which annoys people who see this as crossing Christ out of Christmas. But did you know that X is the first letter— chi (pronounced "kie")—of the Greek word Christos, meaning Anointed One, or Messiah? X-mas is simply an abbreviation for Christmas. (By the way, have you ever noticed how we often use the letter X to mean "cross," as in Railroad X-ing?) Even so, I think it is a good idea to say—or write—the wonderful name of Jesus Christ whenever we can!

But "Merry Christmas!" is still the definitive greeting. Merry, a word we don't often hear today, means "pleasant" or "joyful." It's a lot like the word happy, but merry has a twinkle in its eye. The word Christmas comes from the Old English Cristes Maesse, meaning the feast or mass of Christ. At such a worship service or mass, people take bread and wine and celebrate the Lord's Supper.

Doesn't that seem a little strange? Perhaps out of place? Why would we remember the death of our Lord Jesus on His birthday? And how can we go on exchanging cards that basically say, "Joyfully remember the crucifixion of Jesus!"?

It's really pretty simple. Without the cross, Christ couldn't defeat death. And without His resurrection, there wouldn't be a reason to celebrate. Anything. Ever. With that in mind, this season let's say loudly and often, "Merry Christmas!"

Feliz Navidad · Mele Kalikimaka

Buon Natale · Gesëinde Kersfees · Joyeux Noël

Suk San Wan Christmas

Sheng Tan Kuai Lok

Holiday Greetings

© jeannie mooney

Merry Christmas · Maligayang Pasko

Christmas Is Merry in Any Language!
Teach your child how to say "Merry Christmas" in a dozen languages.

Italian
Buon Natale
(bwon nuh-tall-ā)

Maltese
Il-Milied It-Tajjeb
(il-millit it-tī-yup)

Afrikaans
Geseënde Kersfees
(gĕ-see-end-dĕ kurs-feez)

Polynesian
Ia Orana no te Noere
(yo-rah-nah noh tay noh-ay-ray)

Hungarian
Boldog Kara'csonyt
(bahl-dah kah-rī chah-nyew)

Peace

Hawaiian
Mele Kalikimaka
(meh-leh kah-lee-kee-mah-kah)

Thai
Suk San Wan Christmas
(sook săn wăn krees-mahs)

French
Joyeux Noël
(joh-wah nō-ĕl)

Chinese
Sheng Tan Kuai Lob
(shung tahn kwī lŭb)

Spanish
Feliz Navidad
(feh-leez nah-vee-dah)

Tagalog
Maligayang Pasko
(mah-lee-gī-yong păs-kō)

Swiss-German
Schone Weinachten
(shōn wī-eh-nahk-tehn)

Feliz Navidad · Mele Kalikimaka

Suk San Wan Christmas

Buon Natale · Gesëinde Kersfees · Joyeux Noël

Sheng Tan Kuai Loe

TEACHABLE MOMENTS

- *"When I wish you a 'Merry Christmas,' what do you think I mean?"*

  (Explain the original meaning of the phrase and talk about where it came from.)

- *"Why do you think some people write 'Christmas' with an X, like 'X-mas'?"*

  (Show how the Greek letter X stands for "Christ" in the word *Christmas*.)

- *"What are some other things we can celebrate at Christmas beside Jesus' birth?"*

  (Talk about being thankful for the many reasons Jesus came to earth.)

OUTDOOR LIGHTS

In 1882, only three short years after Thomas Edison patented his invention of the first lightbulb, a friend of his was already hanging strings of lights on a Christmas tree.

That man's name was Edward Johnson. Powered by a simple electric motor hidden under the floor, his Christmas tree rotated six times a minute. The tree had eighty lights in all, each encased in a delicate painted glass bulb. With each turn, the tree alternated colors—red, white, and blue—resulting in a dazzling display of American ingenuity.

Thirteen years later, President Grover Cleveland flipped a switch to light up a huge tree at the White House. By the turn of the century, department stores had begun decorating their exteriors with colored lights, hoping to draw customers like moths to a streetlamp. (It worked, by the way.)

After World War II, American families could also afford to decorate the roofs of their homes with Christmas lights. And you know how that goes! If the Thomases have colored lights on their eaves, the O'Malleys won't be far behind. Entire neighborhoods began to illuminate the night sky with color.

Decorating our homes with Christmas lights is symbolic of what we, as Christians, need to do year-round. Jesus said, "You are the light of the world—like a city on a mountain, glowing in the night for all to see. In the same way, let your good deeds shine out for all to see, so that everyone will praise your heavenly Father" (Matthew 5:14, 16).

However many Christmas lights adorn your home, remember that, like those lights, you have the ability to pierce the world's darkness. Jesus has instructed us to let His light shine, not through electric icicles and flashy displays, but in the very windows of our lives. And not just at Christmas, but every day of the year.

Luminaries

Making homemade luminaries is easy to do and a beautiful way to shine in your neighborhood.

What you'll need:

- Brown or colored paper lunch sacks
- Hole punch (star- and snowflake-shaped punches would be nice)
- Sand or kitty litter
- Votive candles

Directions:

1. Punch numerous holes or shapes in patterns across the sides of each bag.
2. Fill the bottom of each bag with an inch of sand or kitty litter.
3. Anchor a votive candle firmly in the sand and light its wick.
4. "Let there be light!"

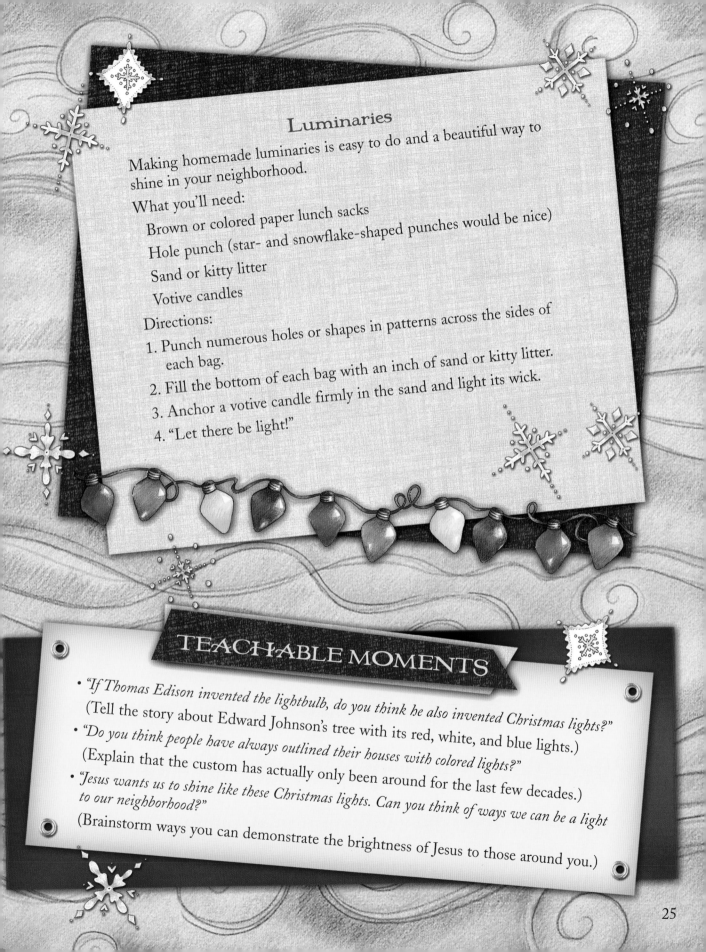

TEACHABLE MOMENTS

- "If Thomas Edison invented the lightbulb, do you think he also invented Christmas lights?" (Tell the story about Edward Johnson's tree with its red, white, and blue lights.)
- "Do you think people have always outlined their houses with colored lights?" (Explain that the custom has actually only been around for the last few decades.)
- "Jesus wants us to shine like these Christmas lights. Can you think of ways we can be a light to our neighborhood?" (Brainstorm ways you can demonstrate the brightness of Jesus to those around you.)

When we think of Christmas, we often paint a picture in our minds with strokes of green and red against a canvas of white, with a touch of silver and gold here and there. Why are these colors most commonly associated with Christmas? Who was the first artist to choose these hues from their palette? It was God. It is He who paints the seasons with colors.

Think about it. Which colors come to mind when someone mentions Easter? Azalea pink, lavender iris, buttercup yellow? The most common colors of springtime in bloom. The same is true for Thanksgiving, when we decorate with pumpkin orange, roasted-turkey brown, and maple-leaf red. At Christmastime, God decorates the world with splashes of holly and berries set against a backdrop of snow—with a flash of the sun reflected in an icicle, just for dramatic effect.

God uses the language of color to help His people understand eternal truths. "Come now, let us reason together,' says the LORD. 'Though your sins are like scarlet, they shall be as white as snow; though they are red as crimson, they shall be like wool'" (Isaiah 1:18, NIV).

Over the years, tradition has ascribed special meaning to the colors of Christmas. Green suggests life—the eternal "ever-green" life we have in Christ. Red recalls the blood that Jesus shed on the cross for us. White speaks of the purity of the spotless Lamb. Gold celebrates the divine nature of God's Son and reminds us that He is the great King. Silver commemorates the price that was paid for His betrayal—and our redemption from the kingdom of darkness into the kingdom of light.

As we decorate this Christmas, let the green of the wreath, the red of the poinsettia, the white of the snowman, the gold of the trumpet, and the silver of the tinsel remind us of the Master Painter and prompt us to praise Him for His creative use of color in our world.

TEACHABLE MOMENTS

- *"Why do you think we decorate with red and green at Christmas?"* (Point out the most common colors found in nature during this season.)
- *"What colors come to mind when you think about Easter? Thanksgiving? Summer? Saint Patrick's Day? Valentine's Day?"* (Keep on going for as long as your child is responding and having fun.) (Talk about God as the Master Painter and think of all the different colors He uses in nature.)
- *"Do you think colors mean anything?"* (Beginning with colors in the Bible and the Christmas colors, talk about other colors and what meanings they might suggest.)

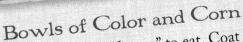

Bowls of Color and Corn

Popcorn is always fun to make and even "funner" to eat. Coat it with sugar and dye it with color, and that's the "funnerest" of all!

Ingredients:

Nonstick cooking spray

14 x 20-inch oven cooking bag

16 cups popped popcorn

2 cups granulated sugar

½ cup light corn syrup

1 teaspoon baking soda

1 teaspoon salt

2 teaspoons almond extract

Red or green *paste* food coloring

Directions:

1. Spray the inside of a 14 x 20-inch oven cooking bag with nonstick cooking spray. Place the popped popcorn in the bag.

2. In a 2-quart microwave-safe bowl, combine the sugar and corn syrup. Microwave until the mixture boils, about two minutes, then stir and microwave for two minutes longer. Stir in the baking soda, salt, and almond extract. Tint the sugar mixture red or green. (Use one color only per batch.)

3. Pour the hot syrup over the popcorn in the bag; twist the top shut and shake until well coated. Microwave for three minutes, stirring and shaking after each minute.

4. Spread the popcorn out over a large sheet of aluminum foil that you've sprayed with nonstick cooking spray. Cool to room temperature, then transfer to an air-tight storage container (that is, if there's any left after the neighborhood kids find out how cool the mom in your house is!).

ANGELS

Angels are everywhere, especially at Christmastime. One may be floating atop your Christmas tree, while a small chorus of angels hovers on your fireplace mantel. Your child may bring home a handmade angel from school. Angels must love to shop, because they always seem to be hanging in department-store windows this time of year.

Angels were hanging all around on that very first Christmas, too. First, the angel Gabriel appeared to a young girl named Mary, proclaiming the news that she would be the mother of the Messiah, God's Son. An angel also appeared to Joseph, Mary's future husband, to assure him that this unexpected baby Mary was expecting was part of God's good and perfect plan.

Nine months later, a whole sky full of angels delivered a living birth announcement to a startled group of shepherds keeping watch over their sheep in the fields. A single angel could easily have delivered the message, but the joyful Father chose to send an army of them. So the night sky rolled back, the light of heaven poured over the land, and the heavenly heralds declared the good news that, after generations of hopeful expectation, the Messiah had been born!

Angels worship God, and Christmas is the perfect opportunity to join them in their jubilant exaltation. Some of the happiest times of the season occur in the midst of festive Christmas parties and holiday entertaining. The food, faith, friends, and fun seem to fill us up with the joy of the occasion. Have you thought of inviting a neighbor to your home, or someone who doesn't have a family with whom to celebrate?

You may be thinking, *Hey, I thought we were talking about angels.* We are. Hebrews 13:2 lets us in on a little secret: "Don't forget to show hospitality to strangers, for some who have done this have entertained angels without realizing it!"

Wouldn't it be fun to have a real angel in your home this Christmas?

Well, you never know....

Be merry

My Little Angel

This Christmas angel has a footprint body and two handprint wings.

1. Have your child stand on a piece of white card stock, poster board, or craft foam and trace around one bare foot. (This will be the robe of the angel.)

2. To form the wings, trace both of your child's hands on yellow paper, or use yellow paint to make a handprint. (You will find that it is easier to cut and the wings look better if the fingers aren't spread too far apart.)

3. Cut out the footprint and decorate the "robe" with glitter, scraps of shiny wrapping paper, silver tinsel, colored tissue paper, or tinfoil.

4. Glue a piece of ribbon accross the center of the robe (this is the belt).

5. Cut out a picture of your child to serve as the angel's head. (Your child's foot size will determine how close-up the face in the photo needs to be.)

6. Assemble the angel: Glue the hand silhouettes to the back of the footprint, then glue your child's photo to the heel. Add yarn for hair and a pipe cleaner for a halo, if desired. (I guess this depends on what kind of day it has been.)

7. Don't forget to record the date and include your child's "signature" on the back, so that you'll remember what an angel your child was this Christmas.

The Invisible Angel

Set aside one day this holiday season for your family to be invisible angels. Explain to your children that the Bible describes angels as servants. Challenge your "little angels" to perform as many random acts of service as possible for each other, their friends, and their neighbors—without getting caught! This game helps children experience the joy of serving others even if nobody notices.

TEACHABLE MOMENTS

- *"Can you think of any time when angels showed up at the first Christmas?"*

  (Share the story of Gabriel and the sky full of angels sent to the shepherds.)

- *"Do you think we can talk to angels today?"*

  (Explain that because we can go directly to Jesus in prayer, we don't need— and shouldn't try—to talk to angels.)

- *"What are some of the ways we could unintentionally serve angels?"*

  (Talk about practical ways you could show hospitality to strangers.)

CANDLES

Have you ever wondered why we put candles in the windows at Christmastime? Wonder no more. During the seventeenth century, the British conquerors of Ireland implemented harsh laws aimed at eradicating Irish traditions. Irishmen were forbidden to vote, send their children to school, purchase land, or own a horse worth more than twenty-five dollars. Irish priests were driven out of the land and warned never to return under penalty of death.

On Christmas Eve, despite the iron hand of their conquerors, Irish families of faith placed a single candle in each of three windows—or three candles in one window—to represent Joseph, Mary, and Jesus. These candles signaled to a traveling priest that the doors were unlocked and he was welcome to come in, share a meal with the family, and celebrate "Christ-mass."

These Irish believers understood that, in the words of the apostle John, Jesus is the Light that shines through the darkness, "and the darkness can never extinguish it" (John 1:5). No matter how many laws are enacted to try to snuff out the gathering of the saints, such laws are no match for the Light of the World!

Crayon Candles

What you will need:

Quart-size milk carton (empty)
Old crayons
Taper candle or wick
Crushed ice

Directions:

1. Cut off the top of the milk carton so you have a box with one end open.
2. Unwrap paper from the crayons and place the crayons in a Ziploc freezer bag.
3. Place the bag in a pan of boiling water (to melt the crayons).
4. Place the tapered candle or wick in the center of milk carton and surround with crushed ice; fill to the top of the carton.
5. Carefully pour the melted crayon mixture into the carton, filling to the top.
6. Let sit until the wax is hardened and the ice has melted.
7. Carefully cut and peel away the carton from the candle.
8. Transfer your "Swiss cheese" candle carefully to a candle holder or dish, and light in a safe place for all to see.

The Darkness Runs Away

Take a flashlight and your child into a closet and turn out the light. Now switch on the flashlight. This powerful demonstration of how Jesus, the Light of the World, overcomes the darkness in the world is one your child will never forget.

TEACHABLE MOMENTS

- *"Have you noticed that some houses have candles in their windows? Have you ever wondered why?"*

  (Share the history of the Irish persecution and what the candles in the windows signaled.)

- *"Do you think the Catholic people were wrong to disobey the government and welcome the priests?"*

  (Talk about the importance of obeying the laws of the land, but the even greater importance of obeying God as the final authority.)

- *"In what ways is Jesus like a candle in the darkness?"*

  (Explain that Jesus is so good that evil can't stand to be around Him, the same way that darkness can't stay when the light shows up.)

CHRISTMAS CARDS

We don't know exactly why Sir Henry Cole created a special card and mailed it to a friend right before Christmas. But he sure started something big!

Fellow Englishman J. C. Horsely recognized a good idea when he saw one, and in 1843 he was the first to sell Christmas cards. He promptly sold out of the one thousand cards he had printed, and London was abuzz with excitement. What a great idea, sending a Christmas greeting through the mail!

History shows that Horsely's timing was perfect. Not even five years before, it would have cost a commoner an entire day's wages to send such a card. But Sir Rowland Hill had come along with a stunning innovation: the penny post. He suggested that the government could save a king's ransom by selling tiny square stickers for a penny as prepayment for the delivery of a letter. This wild idea actually worked, and the Queen promptly knighted him.

From the beginning, these early cards were illustrated with Nativity scenes, Christmas themes, and colorful images of warm family hearths. The words inside the cards echoed the very first Christmas message delivered directly from heaven (and with no need of the penny post): "Behold, I bring you good tidings of great joy which will be to all people" (Luke 2:10, NKJV).

Hearts are especially tender this time of year. There is something about the season that nudges people toward openness to the Good News. No matter how our culture has sought to empty the holiday of its true meaning, it has only succeeded in revealing empty hearts—hearts that long for a transcendent hope and for enduring relationships.

Jesus told His disciples, "Peace be with you. As the Father has sent me, so I send you" (John 20:21). By sending Christmas cards that specifically focus on the Good News of His coming—and the hope of eternal life by trusting in Him—we are able to reach near and far with a message that can change lives and homes forever.

And all for the cost of a tiny square sticker.

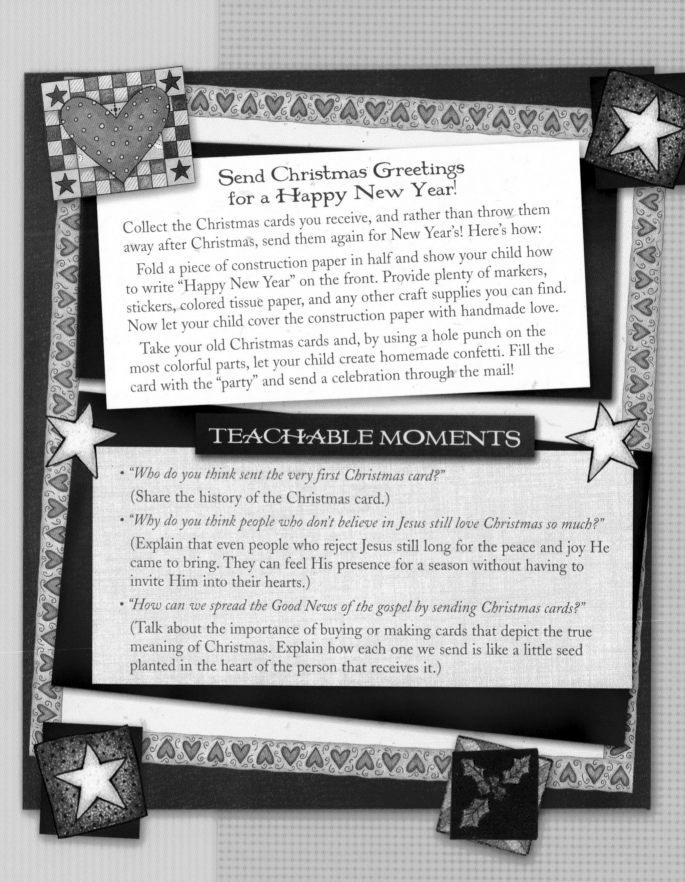

Send Christmas Greetings for a Happy New Year!

Collect the Christmas cards you receive, and rather than throw them away after Christmas, send them again for New Year's! Here's how:

Fold a piece of construction paper in half and show your child how to write "Happy New Year" on the front. Provide plenty of markers, stickers, colored tissue paper, and any other craft supplies you can find. Now let your child cover the construction paper with handmade love.

Take your old Christmas cards and, by using a hole punch on the most colorful parts, let your child create homemade confetti. Fill the card with the "party" and send a celebration through the mail!

TEACHABLE MOMENTS

- *"Who do you think sent the very first Christmas card?"*

  (Share the history of the Christmas card.)

- *"Why do you think people who don't believe in Jesus still love Christmas so much?"*

  (Explain that even people who reject Jesus still long for the peace and joy He came to bring. They can feel His presence for a season without having to invite Him into their hearts.)

- *"How can we spread the Good News of the gospel by sending Christmas cards?"*

  (Talk about the importance of buying or making cards that depict the true meaning of Christmas. Explain how each one we send is like a little seed planted in the heart of the person that receives it.)

A Hug Through the Mail

There is nothing sweeter than a card handmade by a child, unless it is a card with the child's hands inside—reaching out to give a hug.

What you will need:

4 sheets of typing paper

One 14x7-inch sheet of construction paper

Scissors

Markers, crayons, stickers, etc.

Transparent tape

White craft glue

Directions:

1. Tape the 4 sheets of typing paper together, end to end. Lay the paper on the floor or table and trace around your child's hand and arm to cover half of the paper. On the opposite end of the paper, trace around the other hand and arm. Connect the two tracings in the center with lines.

2. Write a message across the arms.

3. Accordion-fold the arms until one hand stacks on the other.

4. Fold a 14x7-inch piece of construction paper in half. Decorate the outside of the card.

5. Attach the hug inside the card by gluing the bottom hand on the right side of the card.

6. Send the card to someone in need of a hug.

BAKING

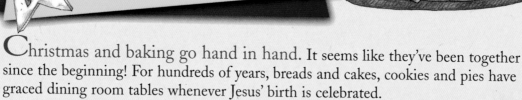

Christmas and baking go hand in hand. It seems like they've been together since the beginning! For hundreds of years, breads and cakes, cookies and pies have graced dining room tables whenever Jesus' birth is celebrated.

Long ago, Christmas Eve was a day of fasting. As a way of preparing themselves for Christmas, people didn't eat anything the entire day, so they were extremely hungry when they woke up on Christmas Day. For breakfast, porridge—a hot, thick, bland cereal—was served.

As time went on, creative wives and mothers began adding dried fruits, spices, and honey to the porridge to make it a special Christmas morning treat. With all these extras, the mixture was thick and stiff, so the cooks wrapped it in a cloth and dunked it in a big pot of boiling water.

Voila! Christmas pudding!

Sometime during the sixteenth century, wheat flour replaced the porridge. Eggs were added to hold the ingredients together, and the resulting treat became known as boiled plum cake. The English used the word *plum* to mean any dried fruit, so what we actually have here is the advent of fruitcake. (And I have a feeling there may be a few of the original fruitcakes still kicking around in the back of someone's pantry.)

When the terms "bread" and "cake" became interchangeable, they called it fruit bread. At one point, ginger was added in remembrance of the gifts of the Magi. (Does this make fruitcake and gingerbread cousins?)

The word *Bethlehem*, which is the birthplace of Jesus, literally means "house of bread." In that humble town in Judea, a baby boy was born who would come to be known as the Bread of Life (see John 6:51). He nourishes us with hope and healing, with forgiveness and love. When you're in the home of a family who loves Jesus, you can almost smell it in the air—just as you can smell bread baking in the oven!

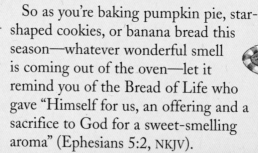

So as you're baking pumpkin pie, star-shaped cookies, or banana bread this season—whatever wonderful smell is coming out of the oven—let it remind you of the Bread of Life who gave "Himself for us, an offering and a sacrifice to God for a sweet-smelling aroma" (Ephesians 5:2, NKJV).

Easy Fruitcake

This is a fun recipe that doesn't require any cooking—just lots of measuring and mixing. Your kids will love making it (even if they don't enjoy eating it).

Ingredients:

½ teaspoon allspice

1 teaspoon cinnamon

½ teaspoon ground cloves

½ teaspoon nutmeg

½ teaspoon salt

½ cup candied cherries

1½ cups chopped dates

1 cup glazed pineapple, diced

½ cup white raisins

1 cup mixed candied fruit

2 cups chopped nuts

2 cups miniature marshmallows

16 ounces finely crushed graham crackers (or use store-bought crumbs)

2 cups heavy whipping cream

Directions:

1. Combine all ingredients *except* the graham cracker crumbs and whipping cream in a mixing bowl; stir together thoroughly.

2. In a separate large mixing bowl, whip the cream until stiff peaks form. Add the fruit mixture to the whipped cream, then fold in the graham cracker crumbs using your hands to mix. (Did you mention to your children how important it is to wash your hands before cooking?) Line a bread pan with tinfoil and press the mixture into the pan. Chill in the refrigerator.

TEACHABLE MOMENTS

- *"Why do you think we bake more at Christmastime?"*
  (Share the story about Christmas Eve originally being a day of fasting before the feasting.)

- *"Do you know how fruitcake got its name?"*
  (Describe how fruitcake started out as plum pudding.)

- *"What would make us think of Jesus when we smell bread baking?"*
  (Talk about Jesus calling Himself the "Bread of Life" and his birthplace being "the house of bread.")

CAROLING

The word *carol*—and there are so many wonderful Christmas carols—has its roots in Greek (*choros*, "the dance," and *aulein*, "to play the flute") and French (*caroller*, "to dance in a ring"). The word originally referred to dancing in a circle accompanied by the flute.

In the early thirteenth century, friar Francis of Assisi introduced carols into formal worship when he held a midnight Mass in a cave in Italy. He encouraged the townspeople to "tell of your Christmas joy in song." (Before then church music was very somber. In fact, the more serious the music, the holier it was considered!) It is said that the worshipers left Mass that night joyfully singing the songs, which then became popular throughout Europe. That's why Francis is considered the father of Christmas carols.

When you think of caroling, do you picture men in top hats and women in velvet cloaks singing about Jesus as they stand under an old-fashioned gas lamp with snow falling softly around them? Or maybe you imagine carolers singing in your own neighborhood, possibly even stopping at your house for a cup of wassail. (This is your imagination, remember?)

We don't have to dress up in fancy clothes, sing like a nightingale, or even know how to *spell* "wassail," much less make it. We just need to gather our family together, go outside, and raise our voices to the rooftops! The tradition of caroling door-to-door is such a moving picture of the power of Christmas. Many who may never cross the threshold of a church will open the door of their home to welcome carolers. And although they may not yet believe that Jesus was born the Son of God, they will, for a season, praise His glorious name in song.

TEACHABLE MOMENTS

- *"Do you know who sang the first Christmas carol?"*
  (Tell the story about Francis of Assisi, the "Father of Christmas carols.")
- *"What do you think is the difference between a Christmas song and a carol?"*
  (Talk about the distinctions between songs like "Jingle Bells" and "Silent Night.")
- *"Why do you think Jesus might smile when He hears us singing Christmas carols?"*
  (Explain how people who may not normally worship God will sing praise songs to Him at Christmastime through carols.)

Silly Seasonal Synonym Songs

Work together and see if your family can guess these common Christmas songs and carols from silly synonym sentences.

1. Move hitherward the entire assembly of those who are loyal in their belief. ("O Come, All Ye Faithful")

2. Small municipality in Judea southeast of Jerusalem. ("O Little Town of Bethlehem")

3. Listen, the celestial messengers produce harmonious sounds. ("Hark, the Herald Angels Sing")

4. Nocturnal time-span of unbroken quietness. ("Silent Night")

5. An emotion excited by the acquisition or expectation of good given to the terrestrial sphere. ("Joy to the World")

6. Embellish the interior passageways. ("Deck the Halls")

7. Diminutive masculine master of skin-covered percussion cylinders. ("Little Drummer Boy")

8. Obese personification fabricated of compressed mounds of minute crystals. ("Frosty the Snowman")

9. Expectation of arrival to populated area by mythical masculine perennial gift-giver. ("Santa Claus Is Coming to Town")

10. The first-person nominative plural of a triumvirate of Far Eastern heads of state. ("We Three Kings")

11. Tintinnabulation of vacillating pendulums in inverted metallic, resonant cups. ("Jingle Bells")

12. In a distant location the existence of an improvised unit of newborn children's slumber furniture. ("Away in a Manger")

sing ◆ Glory to the newborn King

Hark, the herald angels

A ◆ men

THE 12 DAYS OF CHRISTMAS

I know you've heard of Christmas cookies and Christmas carols, but have you ever heard of Christmas code? It just may be that the song "The Twelve Days of Christmas" is really about more than partridges and golden rings.

For nearly three hundred years, it was against the law in England to be a member of the Catholic church. Well, that didn't keep Catholic parents from wanting to teach their children about God, but in order to do so they had to be creative.

And here, once again, is where we leave the world of certain history and move into the misty realms of legend. As the story goes, several of these concerned parents got together and wrote "The Twelve Days of Christmas." They used a secret code hidden in the song to teach their children about the things of God. Let me crack the code for you!

"My true love" represents God, who gives all the gifts listed in the song.

"A partridge in a pear tree" is Jesus, who gave His life on a tree (the cross).

"Two turtle doves" symbolize the Old and New Testaments.

"Three French hens" are faith, hope, and love.

"Four calling birds" speak of the four Gospels: Matthew, Mark, Luke, and John.

"Five golden rings" correspond to the first five books of the Bible, also known as the Pentateuch.

"Six geese a-laying" stand for the six days of creation.

"Seven swans a-swimming" are the seven gifts of the Spirit (Romans 12:6–8).

"Eight maids a-milking" point to the eight beatitudes (Matthew 5:3–10).

"Nine ladies dancing" signify the nine fruits of the Spirit (Galatians 5:22–23).

"Ten lords a-leaping" represent the Ten Commandments.

"Eleven pipers piping" are the eleven faithful disciples. And finally…

"Twelve drummers drumming" call to mind the twelve points of the Apostle's Creed.

Learning this song would help the children remember some important facts about Christianity. Best of all, they could sing it publicly! When they did, they declared their allegiance to the King of kings.

Catechism Concentration

For younger kids:

On twelve index cards, write out the first twelve ordinal numbers: 1st, 2nd, 3rd, etc.

On twelve more cards, list the gifts given on each day in the song: partridge in a pear tree, turtle doves, French hens, etc.

Turn the cards over, mix them up, and have your child turn over two cards at a time, trying to match up the day of Christmas with the gifts given.

For older kids:

On twelve index cards, list the gifts given in the original song: partridge in a pear tree, turtle doves, French hens, etc.

On twelve more cards, list the hidden meanings: Jesus, the Old and New Testaments, faith/hope/love, etc.

Play the same game and help them memorize the Twelve Days' code.

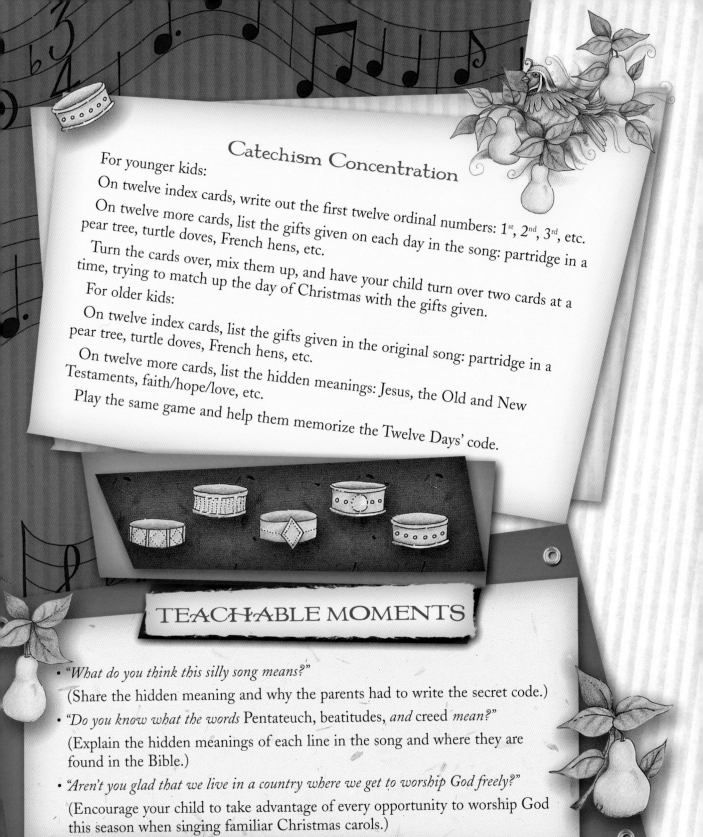

TEACHABLE MOMENTS

- *"What do you think this silly song means?"*

  (Share the hidden meaning and why the parents had to write the secret code.)

- *"Do you know what the words* Pentateuch, beatitudes, *and* creed *mean?"*

  (Explain the hidden meanings of each line in the song and where they are found in the Bible.)

- *"Aren't you glad that we live in a country where we get to worship God freely?"*

  (Encourage your child to take advantage of every opportunity to worship God this season when singing familiar Christmas carols.)

WRAPPING GIFTS

The tradition of giving gifts is as old as Christmas, but wrapping them is a fairly recent development. In seventeenth-century Germany, gifts were rudimentarily wrapped and called "Christ bundles." These packages were stuffed with sugar plums, cakes, candy, apples, and nuts. Most likely it was Mother doing the wrapping, because the packages almost always contained something educational—ABC tables, pencils, or books. Father must have added the finishing touches, because laced up in a ribbon was a "Christ rod"—a pointed little reminder to be good all year long.

Prior to the Victorian Age, most gifts were handmade. Around the late 1800s, however, many people began purchasing and giving "gewgaws and gimcracks," inexpensive, factory-made trinkets. Removing the price tag reduced some of the stigma of giving a store-bought gift...but not completely. You could buy off-the-shelf presents if you had to, but homemade gifts were always the real deal.

Wrapping the bargain in simple brown paper was a step in the right direction. Then, by gluing on dried flowers, spangles, or a clipping from *The Ladies' Home Journal and Practical Housekeeper* magazine, the package was complete.

Why go to so much trouble when "It's the thought that counts"? Or is the saying, "It's what's *inside* that counts"? Truisms graduate to clichés for a reason—because they are true. And these two clichés were never truer than when describing the very first Christmas gift, which came wrapped in swaddling clothes.

"Good things come in small packages." Or would that be "God things come in small packages"? This was God Himself wrapped in the form of a baby! The Bible underscores this unimaginable truth: "Though he was God, he did not demand and cling to his rights as God. He made himself nothing; he took the humble position of a slave and appeared in human form" (Philippians 2:6–7). The greatest gift of all was wrapped in human flesh so that He might be able to wrap all humanity in his outstretched arms of love.

Wrap Wrelay

This is a fun game to play at a children's Christmas party.

1. Divide the children into teams and line them up.
2. Place two stacks of wrapped presents across the room or yard.
3. Place a garbage bag beside each stack.
4. Say, "On your mark, get set, go!"
5. The child at the head of each line runs to pick up a present, unwraps it, throws the paper away, and races back to tag the next child in line.
6. The first team to unwrap all of the presents without leaving any paper lying around wins!
7. Actually, everybody wins because now that they're opened, it's time to enjoy the presents!

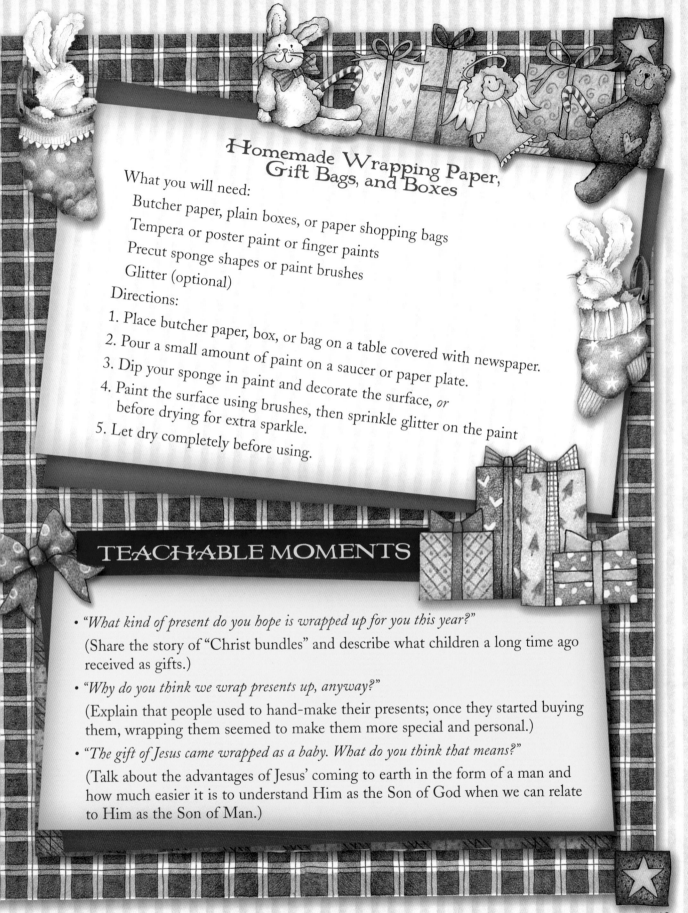

Homemade Wrapping Paper, Gift Bags, and Boxes

What you will need:

Butcher paper, plain boxes, or paper shopping bags

Tempera or poster paint or finger paints

Precut sponge shapes or paint brushes

Glitter (optional)

Directions:

1. Place butcher paper, box, or bag on a table covered with newspaper.
2. Pour a small amount of paint on a saucer or paper plate.
3. Dip your sponge in paint and decorate the surface, *or*
4. Paint the surface using brushes, then sprinkle glitter on the paint before drying for extra sparkle.
5. Let dry completely before using.

TEACHABLE MOMENTS

- *"What kind of present do you hope is wrapped up for you this year?"*

  (Share the story of "Christ bundles" and describe what children a long time ago received as gifts.)

- *"Why do you think we wrap presents up, anyway?"*

  (Explain that people used to hand-make their presents; once they started buying them, wrapping them seemed to make them more special and personal.)

- *"The gift of Jesus came wrapped as a baby. What do you think that means?"*

  (Talk about the advantages of Jesus' coming to earth in the form of a man and how much easier it is to understand Him as the Son of God when we can relate to Him as the Son of Man.)

GIVING GIFTS

Stay warm and cozy!

Many believe that the custom of giving gifts at Christmas began with the wise men, who came to Bethlehem bearing lavish gifts for the Christ child. Is it true?

Well, yes and no.

Why did these powerful, learned men journey across the wide world to give extravagant presents to a child? Because Someone else gave first. God had already given the world the incomprehensible gift of His own Son.

Perhaps the most famous verse in the Bible, John 3:16, explains why God gave such a gift: "For God so loved the world that he gave his only Son, so that everyone who believes in him will not perish but have eternal life." Not coincidentally, *First* John 3:16 tell us, "We know what real love is because Christ gave up his life for us." God gave His Son, and the Son gave His life for us. Giving is the beginning, the end, and the very heart of Christmas.

No wonder we love to shop and buy and extend ourselves throughout the holidays. No wonder we're so willing to sacrifice our time, our money, and our energy searching for that elusive "right gift." Every time we give hugs, baked treats, parties, cards, poinsettias, and smiles, we are presenting God's love to the world—the reason He gave in the first place.

So give and give and give some more, and every chance you have, give to someone as if you were giving to Jesus Himself. Giving is an act of obedience, but it comes with a promise of blessing. Jesus said, "If you give, you will receive. Your gift will return to you in full measure, pressed down, shaken together to make room for more, and running over. Whatever measure you use in giving—large or small—it will be used to measure what is given back to you" (Luke 6:38).

A long time ago, children of Holland would save their pennies all year long in a pig-shaped pot called a "feast pig." (Yep, the ancestor of our piggy bank.) On the day after Christmas, they would break open the pig and give the money to the poor. Giving to those who can't give back is the very best investment because it means the reward you receive will come directly from Jesus. And nobody can ever give more than He gives!

Thank God for his Son—a gift too wonderful for words! (2 Corinthians 9:15)

from your heart

Feast Pig

Give your child a piggy bank this Christmas. Throughout the coming year, feed the "feast pig" coins found on the ground, change given by grandparents, and collected pennies. On the day after next Christmas, you and your child can take the money to a homeless shelter or personally deliver it to a family in need.

Gifts from the Heart, Hand, and Home

Spend a day with your child making gifts for the needy (the emotionally needy, that is.) While you make homemade breads and cookies, your child can hand-make cards and crafts. Together, take them to a local nursing home and ask the director which of the folks won't have any family visiting them this year. Your child will learn firsthand what Jesus meant when He said, "It is more blessed to give than to receive."

TEACHABLE MOMENTS

- *"Why do you think we give gifts at Christmas?"*

   (Quote John 3:16 and apply that to Christmas giving.)

- *"Can you think of ways that God still gives us presents?"*

   (List the many ways—from sunrises, to health, to good jobs, to the privilege of being a mommy!)

- *"How can we give gifts back to Jesus?"*

   (Share Matthew 10:42, about how giving even a cold cup of water in Jesus' name is giving to Jesus. Think of other ways.)

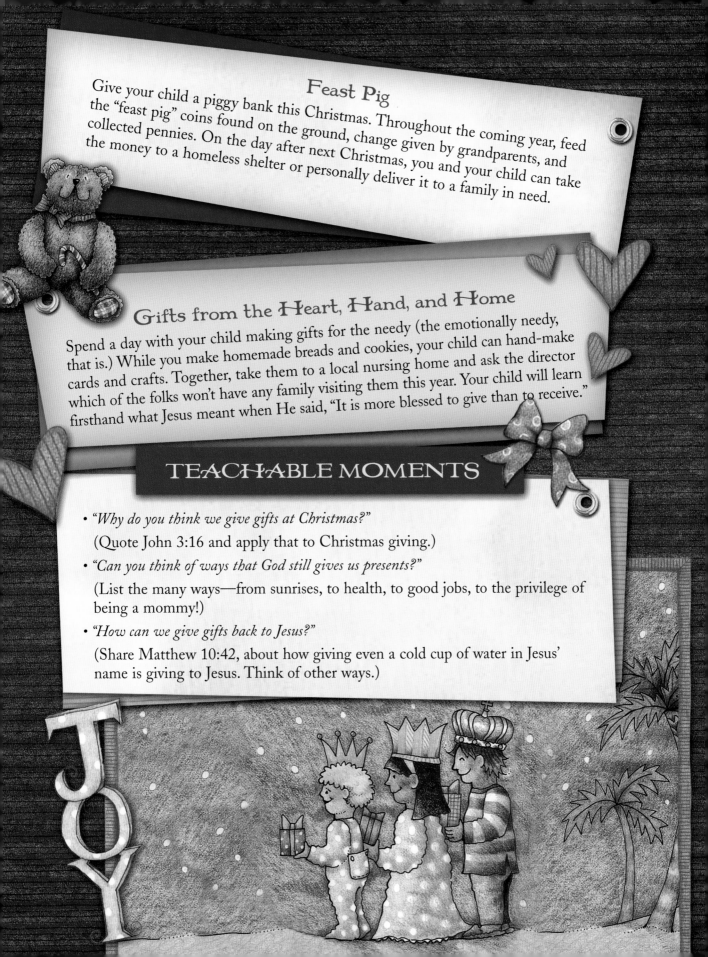

SANTA CLAUS

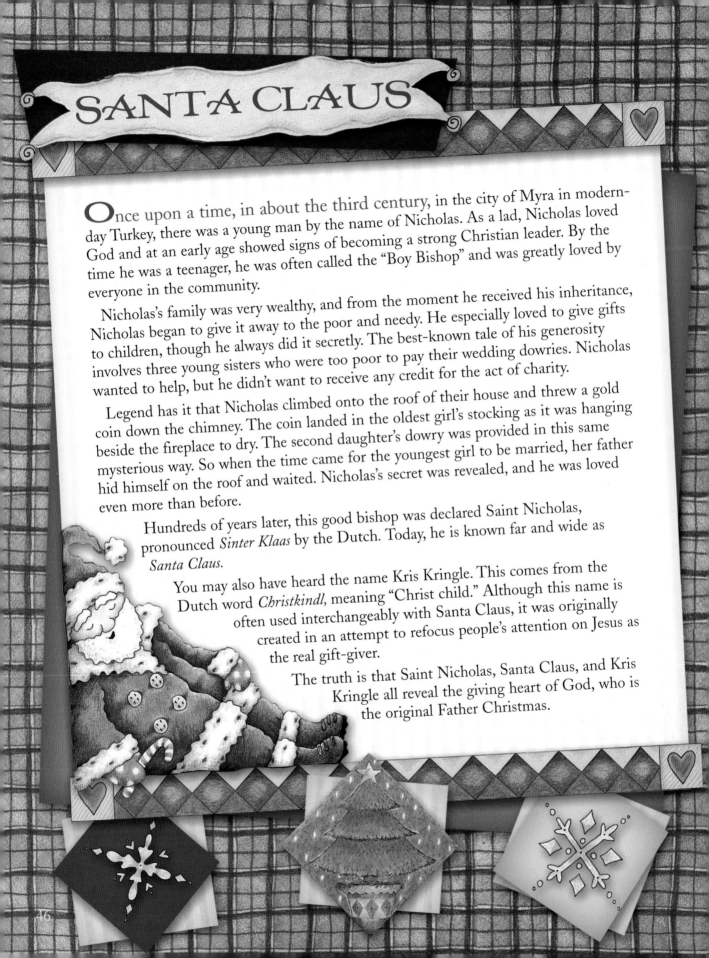

Once upon a time, in about the third century, in the city of Myra in modern-day Turkey, there was a young man by the name of Nicholas. As a lad, Nicholas loved God and at an early age showed signs of becoming a strong Christian leader. By the time he was a teenager, he was often called the "Boy Bishop" and was greatly loved by everyone in the community.

Nicholas's family was very wealthy, and from the moment he received his inheritance, Nicholas began to give it away to the poor and needy. He especially loved to give gifts to children, though he always did it secretly. The best-known tale of his generosity involves three young sisters who were too poor to pay their wedding dowries. Nicholas wanted to help, but he didn't want to receive any credit for the act of charity.

Legend has it that Nicholas climbed onto the roof of their house and threw a gold coin down the chimney. The coin landed in the oldest girl's stocking as it was hanging beside the fireplace to dry. The second daughter's dowry was provided in this same mysterious way. So when the time came for the youngest girl to be married, her father hid himself on the roof and waited. Nicholas's secret was revealed, and he was loved even more than before.

Hundreds of years later, this good bishop was declared Saint Nicholas, pronounced *Sinter Klaas* by the Dutch. Today, he is known far and wide as *Santa Claus.*

You may also have heard the name Kris Kringle. This comes from the Dutch word *Christkindl,* meaning "Christ child." Although this name is often used interchangeably with Santa Claus, it was originally created in an attempt to refocus people's attention on Jesus as the real gift-giver.

The truth is that Saint Nicholas, Santa Claus, and Kris Kringle all reveal the giving heart of God, who is the original Father Christmas.

'Tis the Season to be Jolly

He "Nose" When You're Awake

This game is bound to produce plenty of giggles at your child's party or in your backyard.

What you will need:

Red construction paper
2 jars of Vaseline

Directions:

1. Cut one-inch circles from construction paper to make Santa noses.

2. Divide children into teams and line them up.

3. Place the jars of Vaseline and two plates of noses directly across the room or yard.

4. Call, "On your mark, get set, go!"

5. The first child from each team runs to the Vaseline, applies some to his nose, sticks a Santa nose on the Vaseline, and races back to tag the next team member, who rushes forward to do the same thing. (If the child's nose falls off, the contestant must stop and stick it on again before proceeding.)

6. A good race will end up so close that the winner may be determined "by a nose"!

TEACHABLE MOMENTS

• *"Most people say that Santa lives at the North Pole, but do you know where he came from?"*

(Share the story of Bishop Nicholas.)

• *"Hanging socks on the mantel sure is a strange tradition. Why do you think we do that?"*

(Tell the story of Nicholas and the gold coins tossed down the chimney.)

• *"In what ways does Santa Claus remind you of God, the real Father Christmas?"*

(Compare the qualities of love, generosity, kindness, gift-giving, joy, etc. Now talk about ways that God is even more wonderful than Santa Claus.)

CHRISTMAS PAGEANTS

You might be surprised to learn that the word *pageant* comes from the Middle English word *pagonds*, which means "wagons." You may be wondering, *What in the world does a wagon have to do with Christmas pageants?* Good question. And the answer is delightful.

Medieval dramas were often performed, primarily at Christmas and Easter, on floating stages. (Think Tournament of Roses parade.) These large, two tiered wagons were covered with decorations and flowers. The lower half of the "float" was encased in a curtain and served as a dressing room. The top half was the stage where the holiday pageant was performed.

There were as many floats as there were scenes in the play, and each scene was played by a different "guild," or troupe of actors. The festival began in the morning with Act One, Scene One. The first wagon would pull into the street, and the first troupe would perform their portion of the pageant. When their scene was complete, they would move on to the next street and perform it again for a new crowd, while their previous spot was occupied with the next wagon and the next episode of the sacred drama.

These roving stages would progress through town in a carefully timed procession. While individual scenes were relatively short, it was the multiple intermissions necessary to move the wagons from one site to another that seemed to take all day—and well into the night! Sometimes as long as eighteen hours later, the final curtain would fall (along with a few exhausted actors, I would imagine).

Why go to all this trouble? To reach people where they lived and teach them in their own language. This was the fifteenth century, when most people couldn't read and the church services were all in Latin. These Christmas miracle plays dramatized Jesus' first day on earth. In so doing, they followed the instruction He gave on His last day: Go into all the world and preach the Good News to everyone, everywhere.

Paul wrote, "Thanks be to God, who always leads us in triumphal procession in Christ and through us spreads everywhere the fragrance of the knowledge of him" (2 Corinthians 2:14, NIV). As we travel during these busy holidays—from state to state, store to store, house to house, even room to room—each of us is a movable stage, displaying His life and carrying with us the fragrance of His presence.

Christmas at Our House

Encourage your children to put on their own Christmas pageant. Provide them with sheets and robes for costumes, a doll for baby Jesus, and a cane for the shepherds. And use the family dog as a lamb. Show them how to make crowns out of construction paper and props from items around the house. Set a date, invite Grandma and Grandpa over, and let them put on a show. And don't forget the video camera!

Attend a Christmas Pageant

If your church isn't putting on a Christmas pageant, find one that is and take your children. Some are simple; others are elaborate—music, flying angels, and real animals (along with real animal smells!). See if there is a church in your area producing a "living pageant" with actors who will interact with your children and answers their questions while remaining in character. Christmas plays have a way of making the story come to life in a child's heart. Perhaps you could make it a family tradition to attend a different production every year.

TEACHABLE MOMENTS

- *"Do you think churches always put on Christmas plays?"*

  (Share the history and explain that the first plays were actually performed in the middle of the towns.)

- *"If you had a friend that didn't know Jesus, do you think she would rather come to church to learn about Him, or have you tell her the story?"*

  (Talk about the importance of going into the world to preach the gospel in ways people can understand.)

- *"How can we 'act' like Jesus everywhere we go?"*

  (Explain the concept behind the adage "You may be the only Bible somebody ever reads.")

NATIVITY SCENES

The Nativity scene, also referred to as the *crèche*, or crib, is *the* symbol of Christmas. It illustrates the night of Jesus' birth and the beginning of His-story. But we know that God wrote this story long before the first Christmas Eve.

From the moment when Adam and Eve sinned, mankind was separated from God. This broke the Father's heart, and so immediately He set the plan in motion to send His Son, the Messiah, to restore the Father's relationship with His children—because this relationship is the reason He created us in the first place.

Like any father who has an extra-special present already wrapped and ready to give to his children, God could hardly wait to give the gift of His Son to the world. But just like the dreaded sticker reads, "Do not open 'til Christmas," God chose to wait until the fulfillment of time. That didn't mean He couldn't drop a few hints along the way. Throughout Scripture we see that God revealed bits and pieces of the big surprise to His children. Even not knowing all the details, they knew enough to get excited. Because of this, the children of Israel knew that God was going to send the Messiah to redeem His people. The Scriptures revealed that the child would be born of a virgin, in Bethlehem, and would be a descendant of their beloved King David. Some believe that other Old Testament passages may have pointed to the star of Bethlehem and the gifts of the Magi.

Can you see how many of the pieces in the nativity scene illustrates a fulfillment of prophecy? The stable in Bethlehem, Mary the virgin mother, Joseph the direct descendant of David, the star, the wise men bearing gifts from the East, and, of course, the baby Jesus.

Then the angel said to them, "Do not be afraid, for behold, I bring you good tidings of great joy which will be to all people. For there is born to you this day in the city of David a Savior, who is Christ the Lord. And this will be the sign to you: You will find a Babe wrapped in swaddling cloths, lying in a manger" (Luke 2:10–12, NKJV).

joyous ✦ night

Preparing the Manger

Find a Nativity scene that has a manger with a separate baby Jesus. Set up all the pieces with the exception of the baby Jesus. Gather a handful of straw (or buy some at the craft store). Throughout the season, reward your children for acts of kindness, service, or obedience with a blade of straw. Allow them to place each blade in the empty manger. The goal is to make sure that the Baby Jesus has a comfortable place to rest when you place Him in the manger scene on Christmas Eve.

Who's the Nativity Neighbor?

Buy an inexpensive Nativity scene with lots of individual pieces. Count the number of pieces and, beginning with the stable, work backward from Christmas Eve, secretly leaving one piece at a time at a neighbor's front door. On Christmas Eve, leave the Baby Jesus with a note attached, revealing your family's identity along with warm holiday wishes.

TEACHABLE MOMENTS

- *"What is your favorite decoration in our house? Which one do you think is the most important?"*

  (Show your child why the Nativity scene represents what Christmas is all about better than any other decoration.)

- *"Do you think Christmas is the first time the Bible talks about Jesus?"*

  (Explain that prophecies in the Old Testament talked about the Messiah hundreds of years before the first Christmas. That is one of the ways we could recognize that Jesus was the Messiah.)

- *"Why do you think God sent Jesus to be born in the first place?"*

  (Tell your child that God created us because He wanted to have a relationship with us but our sin kept us too far apart. By sending Jesus, God made a way for us to come back to Him.)

THE WISE MEN

Who ever said there were three of them? Or that they were at the stable with the shepherds? Or that they were even kings? A popular Christmas carol makes its vote clear: "We three kings of Orient are bearing gifts..." The Bible, however, never refers to the Magi as kings, and they most likely journeyed from Persia rather than from what we now think of as the Orient.

Now, before you saw the crowns off your Nativity figurines, you should understand that certain Old Testament prophecies suggest this interpretation. However, when Matthew tells the story, he never calls them kings—and he doesn't call them by name, either.

The Gospel of Matthew refers to these travelers as "wise men" or "Magi," translated from the Greek word *magoi*—from which we get our word *magician*. But don't think card tricks and bunnies pulled from top hats here! These magicians were priests, powerful men of great wealth who counseled the kings of the Medo-Persian Empire.

So where did the "three wise men" story get started? That's likely a presumption based on the fact that three gifts were presented to Jesus. Which brings up yet another misconception. The Magi were not even present in the original manger scene. By the time they brought their baby shower gifts to the party, Jesus was probably close to two years old.

And what strange gifts they were!

Gold? Frankincense? Myrrh? A gold rattle, perhaps, or a little gold baby spoon. But who would bring spices to a toddler? Let's see if we can clear that one up.

Gold signified royalty and acknowledges Christ as the King of kings. Frankincense was used in worship and denotes the deity of Jesus. Myrrh was most commonly used in preparation for burial and represents the death of the Son of Man, who would rise to sit at the right hand of the Father as the Son of God.

Who would give such strange gifts to a baby? Wise men would.

Gift-in-a-Jar

What you'll need:

- 1 cup flour
- 1 teaspoon baking soda
- 1 teaspoon cinnamon
- ½ teaspoon nutmeg
- ½ teaspoon salt
- ¾ cup packed brown sugar
- ½ cup sugar
- ¾ cup raisins
- 2 cups uncooked quick oats
- One quart-size canning jar
- One 6-inch square scrap of fabric
- Ribbon
- Gift tag with handwritten baking instructions*

Directions:

1. Sift flour, baking soda, cinnamon, nutmeg, and salt into a small bowl.

2. Layer the ingredients in the jar in this order: brown sugar first, then sugar, raisins, oats, and flour mixture.

3. As you layer, press each ingredient firmly in place before adding the next.

4. Cut the edges of the fabric square with pinking shears.

5. Lay the fabric on top of the lid and secure it with the ribbon.

6. Copy the baking instructions onto the gift tag (see below) and tie onto ribbon.

7. Journey to a friend's house and present the gift. (Bowing isn't necessary.)

*Baking Instructions for gift tag:

OATMEAL RAISIN SPICE COOKIE MIX

Empty the jar of cookie mix into a large mixing bowl; stir to combine. Add ¾ cup (1½ sticks) softened butter, 1 egg slightly beaten, and 1 teaspoon vanilla; mix until completely blended. Scoop heaping tablespoonfuls of batter and place 2 inches apart on a lightly greased cookie sheet. Bake at 350°F until edges are lightly browned, 11 to 13 minutes. Cool for 5 minutes on cookie sheet; then remove to wire racks to cool completely. Yield: 3 dozen.

TEACHABLE MOMENTS

- *"Who do you think the wise men were and where did they come from?"*
  (Share what we do know about the Magi and talk about how much we don't know.)
- *"What could they have been thinking, to bring gold, frankincense, and myrrh as gifts to a baby?"*
  (Explain what the three gifts symbolized about Jesus' life and future.)
- *"How can we learn from the wise men and become wise?"*
  (Talk about the wisdom of obedience, faith, tenacity, etc., that the Magi exhibited and which we, too, can demonstrate.)

DECEMBER 25th

The Romans called it *Saturnalia,* which means "the birthday of the unconquerable sun," and they celebrated it in a big way! They spent an entire week feasting and worshiping their false gods, and they capped it off with the biggest and wildest party of all. That party was held on December 25th.

But something happened in A.D. 313 that would change everything. Those seven evil days of idol worship and over-the-top parties would disappear from the Roman calendar, and December 25th would move out of the dark shadows of pagan worship into the light of God's truth and love.

How did this happen?

In the year A.D. 313, the Roman emperor Constantine became a follower of Jesus Christ. As a believer, Constantine was disturbed by his people's worship of false gods. Acting on his concern, Constantine declared December 25th the Feast of the Nativity. And when a Roman emperor declares something, it gets done!

In the years that followed, the Feast of the Nativity would become "Christ-mass," which eventually became our Christmas. It shouldn't surprise us that something dark and evil has been transformed into a day characterized by radiant light, selfless giving, and sacrificial love. Romans 12:21 says, "Do not be overcome by evil, but overcome evil with good (NIV)."

More than likely Jesus was not actually born on December 25th. But given the fact that it is around this date that darkness prevails with the year's longest night and the sun begins a new cycle, it's a grand time to celebrate the birthday of the Son. Proclaiming and reclaiming December 25th gives an opportunity for God's light of truth to chase away the blackest of shadows, revealing the true "Sun of Righteousness."

December

Joy to the World the Lord has come

Happy Birthday, Jesus!

What you will need:

- 1 box of white cake mix
- Red, green, and yellow food coloring
- 1 container of white frosting
- Two 8- or 9-inch round cake pans
- 1 large white taper candle
- 1 box of small birthday candles

Directions:

1. Prepare the white cake mix according to directions on the box.
2. Divide the batter evenly between two bowls.
3. Butter and flour the cake pans, tapping out any excess flour.
4. Add several drops of red food coloring (representing the blood of Jesus) to the first bowl of batter. Mix well and pour into the first cake pan.
5. Add several drops of green food coloring (representing eternal life) to the second bowl of batter. Mix well and pour into the second cake pan.
6. Bake the cake layers according to directions on the box.
7. Let cool and then remove from the pans.
8. Add several drops of yellow food coloring (representing the birthday of the Son of Righteousness) to the white frosting.
9. Fill and frost the red and green layers with the yellow frosting.
10. Place the large white taper candle (representing Jesus as the center of our lives) in the middle of the cake.
11. Give each member of the family a small birthday candle (representing our lives revolving around Jesus) and have them place the candles around the perimeter of the cake.
12. Sing "Happy Birthday" to Jesus.
13. Using the "Jesus" candle, light the smaller birthday candles.
14. Say a prayer and blow out the candles!

TEACHABLE MOMENTS

- *"Do you think this is Jesus' real birthday?"*

  (Share why Constantine chose to celebrate Jesus' birthday on December 25.)

- *"Why do you think it is wrong to worship the sun?"*

  (Explain how silly—and sinful—it is to worship creation when we can worship the Creator.)

- *"How can we remember that Jesus is the reason for every season?"*

  (Brainstorm about ways to make Jesus the focus of all our holiday celebrations.)

59

OPENING PRESENTS

Traditions! At no other time of the year are traditions more important than at Christmastime. A tradition is like a secret password that allows you into the club and tells you that you belong to something bigger than yourself. Traditions bind people together as family, church, nation, or culture.

Some Christmas customs and rituals cross cultural lines; others define them. In Australia, Santa's sleigh is pulled by eight white kangaroos. In Finland, it is traditional to take a sauna bath before Santa's visit. In Spain, Papa Noel delivers presents by climbing up balconies. And in New Zealand, Christmas is in summer, so families head to the beach for a yule-"tide" picnic.

When and how to open gifts is another tradition that varies the world over. Should presents be opened on Christmas Eve or Christmas morning? Do you put them under the tree or hide them in the branches? Are they wrapped or unwrapped? One thing is certain: In the end, it doesn't really matter how a present is opened, so long as it is opened.

What if you had put a lot of thought into finding the perfect present to give someone you loved very much? This gift cost you more than anybody could ever know, but to you, this person was worth it. Now how would you feel if the one you adored never opened the gift, or refused to even receive it?

God gave the gift of His Son, Jesus, to you. Have you opened your heart to receive Him as your Savior? The Bible says, "It pleases me that you continue to remember and honor me by keeping up the traditions of the faith I taught you" (1 Corinthians 11:2, *The Message*). This Christmas, it would please the Lord if you would open the gift He has given you.

You don't even have to wait until Christmas.

This Gift Comes with Strings Attached!

Tie a very, very long piece of yarn to one of the wrapped gifts you're giving. Now hide the present. Take a hold of the loose end of the yarn and wrap it around chair legs, through stair banisters, over tables, under couches—all over the house! To make this activity even more fun, hide a present for each member of the family, using a different color of yarn for each person. When it is time to hunt for the presents, just tell each person which color of yarn to follow. Oh, what a tangled web we weave! And what fun it is to hide and seek!

It's All in the Present-ation

Place enough small candy canes for each member of the family, and a single large one, inside a small box and then wrap the box. Put the wrapped box inside a larger box, wrap it, and then select another larger box until you've used all the boxes you can find. Have everyone sit in a circle and pass the package around as you play Christmas music in the background. When the music stops, the player holding the package unwraps it to reveal another wrapped package. Start the music again and continue passing the package around, unwrapping a box every time the music stops. The person opening the final box gets the large candy cane and shares the rest of his gift with everyone else.

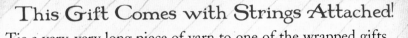

TEACHABLE MOMENTS

- *"What is your favorite Christmas tradition we celebrate as a family?"*
  (Share some of the funny Christmas traditions experienced around the world.)
- *"When do you think is the best time to open presents?"*
  (Share some of the family traditions you and your husband celebrated as children and why you've chosen to celebrate the ones you have for your family.)
- *"How do you think you would feel if you picked out something extra special to give someone you loved and they didn't even open it?"*
  (Talk to your child about how she can open her heart to receive the gift of Jesus.)

CHRISTMAS DINNER

Jesus was always inviting Himself over for a meal—and what a dinner guest He was! You never knew quite what to expect when He stepped through the door. You might witness a miracle between the first course and the second. You might hear, for better or worse, surprising truths about yourself. You might find yourself serving a ragtag cast of characters from the other side of the tracks. One time Jesus even provided the wine—180 gallons of it!

One of His last acts before He died was to break bread with the people closest to Him. Today we remember His death on the cross for our sins when we drink the cup and eat the bread of Communion.

Knowing all this about Jesus, we shouldn't be surprised that the first celebration of His birth was a feast—specifically, the Feast of the Nativity, which originated in Rome during the fourth century. Although there are no records of such a feast in the early church, and you won't find it in the Bible, it isn't out of character with either. The Old Testament brims with feasts designed by God and given to His people. And as we've seen in the New Testament accounts of His life, Jesus loved to eat with His friends. (Sounds like a pretty good endorsement for feasting to me.)

The last book of the Bible, Revelation, tells us that a great banquet will be one of the first things we experience together in heaven. As one angel put it, "Blessed are those who are invited to the wedding feast of the Lamb" (Revelation 19:9). Do you know how to get invited to that party? Jesus said, "Look! Here I stand at the door and knock. If you hear me calling and open the door, I will come in, and we will share a meal as friends" (Revelation 3:20).

As you sit at the table for Christmas dinner and thank God for the food, remember Jesus. If you've never invited Him to step through the door and be Lord of your life, what better time to do it than at Christmas? It's His birthday, and—from then on and forever—it will be yours, too.

A Birthday Invitation

If you feel like your child is ready, why don't you ask if he would like to say this prayer and ask Jesus to come inside and be Lord of his heart and life?

Dear Jesus,

Thank You for coming to earth as a baby that very first Christmas. I believe You are the Son of God and that You came to die on the cross for my sins. I want to receive the gift of forgiveness that You have bought for me. Please come into my heart and be my Lord and Savior. Thank You for loving me so much. I love You, too. Amen.

Christmas Wassail

I can't imagine that Wassail was not served at the very first Feast of the Nativity. Even if it wasn't, we can still serve it at our Christmas feast.

1 gallon apple cider
1 teaspoon ground allspice
1 teaspoon ground cinnamon
1 teaspoon ground cloves
1 teaspoon ground nutmeg
½ cup firmly packed brown sugar
One 6-ounce can of frozen lemonade concentrate, thawed
One 6- ounce can of frozen orange juice concentrate, thawed

Combine 2 cups of the apple cider with the allspice, cinnamon, cloves, and nutmeg in a large Dutch oven; bring to a boil. Reduce heat to low and simmer for 10 minutes. Add the remaining cider, brown sugar, lemonade concentrate, and orange concentrate to the hot mixture, stirring well to dissolve the sugar; heat until very hot (do not boil). Makes 4½ quarts.

TEACHABLE MOMENTS

- *"Do you have any idea why we always eat so much at Christmas?"*

   (Ask your child if she thinks it might be because Jesus enjoyed eating with His family and friends so much. Share some examples of feasting from the Bible.)

- *"Do you think people have been eating big meals at Christmastime from the very beginning?"*

   (Tell your child about the first Christmas dinner, the Feast of the Nativity.)

- *"I hope we get to eat in heaven, how about you?"*

   (Talk about how we get invited to the Wedding Feast of the Lamb in heaven.)

THE CHRISTMAS STORY

At that time the Roman emperor, Augustus, decreed that a census should be taken throughout the Roman Empire. (This was the first census taken when Quirinius was governor of Syria.) All returned to their own towns to register for this census. And because Joseph was a descendant of King David, he had to go to Bethlehem in Judea, David's ancient home. He traveled there from the village of Nazareth in Galilee. He took with him Mary, his fiancée, who was obviously pregnant by this time.

And while they were there, the time came for her baby to be born. She gave birth to her first child, a son. She wrapped him snugly in strips of cloth and laid him in a manger, because there was no room for them in the village inn.

That night some shepherds were in the fields outside the village, guarding their flocks of sheep. Suddenly, an angel of the Lord appeared among them, and the radiance of the Lord's glory surrounded them. They were terribly frightened, but the angel reassured them. "Don't be afraid!" he said. "I bring you good news of great joy for everyone! The Savior—yes, the Messiah, the Lord—has been born tonight in Bethlehem, the city of David! And this is how you will recognize him: You will find a baby lying in a manger, wrapped snugly in strips of cloth!" Suddenly, the angel was joined by a vast host of others—the armies of heaven—praising God:

"Glory to God in the highest heaven,

and peace on earth to all whom God favors."

When the angels had returned to heaven, the shepherds said to each other, "Come on, let's go to Bethlehem! Let's see this wonderful thing that has happened, which the Lord has told us about."

They ran to the village and found Mary and Joseph. And there was the baby, lying in the manger. Then the shepherds told everyone what had happened and what the angel had said to them about this child. All who heard the shepherds' story were astonished, but Mary quietly treasured these things in her heart and thought about them often.

The shepherds went back to their fields and flocks, glorifying and praising God for what the angels had told them, and because they had seen the child, just as the angel had said.

Luke 2:1–20